THE STORY OF
ROME

Rosie Dickins

Illustrated by Teri Gower

Historical consultant: Dr. Verity Platt
Oxford University

Reading consultant: Alison Kelly
Roehampton University

Contents

Chapter 1

The myth of Rome

The city of Rome, in Italy, is over
two thousand years old, and its
beginning is cloaked in mystery.
According to myth, it all started
with twin brothers – Romulus
and Remus.

The twins were royal babies. Their mother was a glamorous princess and their father was Mars, the god of war. They should have inherited a kingdom from their grandfather, King Numitor, and lived happily ever after.

But King Numitor's brother, Amulius, had banished him and stolen the crown. And Amulius didn't want any rivals...

I've got to get rid of them!

"Take those brats to the River Tiber and drown them," he ordered a slave. But the slave took pity on them and sent them floating gently down the river in a basket.

After a while, the basket washed ashore. A wolf heard the boys crying and went to look. Perhaps she thought they were cubs, because she fed and cared for them as if they were her own babies.

5

Soon after this, a shepherd named Faustulus spotted the boys. Faustulus and his wife longed for children. "I'll rescue them, and we can bring them up as our own sons," he decided.

I thought we could call them Romulus and Remus.

Romulus and Remus grew up big, strong – and always ready for a fight. They became shepherds like Faustulus, spending each day in the hills.

One day, Remus got into a brawl with some rival shepherds, who dragged him before a local judge.

"Who's this?" the judge asked. "Where's he from?"

Sulkily, Remus explained how he and his twin had been found as babies. To his astonishment, the judge hugged him.

7

"My boy," the judge cried. "I thought you were dead! It's me — your grandad Numitor." He sent for Romulus and told the brothers all about Amulius.

Romulus and Remus were furious. They stormed off to Amulius's palace, killed him and gave the crown back to Numitor.

Numitor invited his grandsons to stay and rule the city with him. But they missed the hills.

"Let's go back and build a city of our own," Romulus said.

Remus nodded.

The only problem was they couldn't agree where to start. After a lot of bickering, they set to work on different hilltops.

Then Remus looked at Romulus's walls and laughed. "Your walls are useless," he teased. "Look, I can jump over them!"

Ha ha.

Romulus was furious. He lashed out and dealt Remus a terrible blow with his sword. His brother fell down, dead.

So, Romulus finished the city by himself. He named it Rome, after himself, and became its first king.

Welcome to my city.

Romulus gathered together a ragged bunch of outlaws and runaways to fill his city. But they were short of women, so Romulus came up with a sneaky plan.

He invited a tribe known as the Sabines to a great feast. While the Sabine men ate and drank, his men carried off their daughters.

When they woke, the Sabine men wanted revenge. But, to their surprise, the women didn't. They begged the men not to fight. In the end, they persuaded both sides to make peace.

After that, Romulus ruled Rome for many years – until one day, he vanished in a clap of thunder. People said his father, Mars, had taken him to live with the gods.

Chapter 2

The real Rome

Rome wasn't built in a day.

The myth of Romulus and Remus is a good story, but there isn't much evidence for it. Rome can't really have been built by one man. So what did happen?

Historians think shepherds and farmers began to settle on the seven hills where Rome now stands nearly 3,000 years ago.

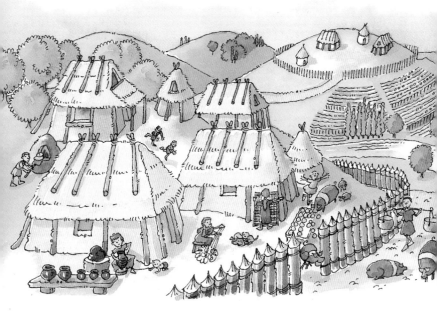

Each family had just a small hut, with a vegetable garden and a few animals. They grew all their own food, and made their own clothes and tools.

The hills were in a good spot by the River Tiber, and easy to defend, so more and more people came to live there...

...until each hilltop had a bustling village. Eventually, the villages joined together to form a city – Rome. And the city-dwellers became known as Romans.

Together, the Romans were able to drain the marshy land between the hills and build a huge stone marketplace known as the Forum.

On top of the highest hill, named the Capitol, they put a temple dedicated to Jupiter, the king of the gods.

Strong defensive walls went up around the city, and sewers were dug to take away its waste.

Life in the city was much easier than on the old farms. People could buy everything they needed in shops.

And they had an army to keep order and defend the city.

Priests and fortune-tellers did good business, too. People paid them to look for signs in the weather or in the bodies of dead animals.

In their spare time they could watch daredevil chariot races at the Circus Maximus.

The city was ruled by a king and a group of wealthy noblemen known as the Senate. The noblemen were called senators. Together, they all decided what the law should be...

...what buildings to put up...

...and when to go to war.

Most of the kings ruled wisely. But one, King Tarquin, was selfish and proud. He ignored the senators and bullied the people.

Then Tarquin's son, Sextus, attacked a senator's wife. It was the last straw. The senators rebelled.

The senators banished Tarquin and Sextus, and began to run Rome themselves. They wrote new laws, organized the army and even allowed some people to vote – as long as they weren't women or slaves.

VOTE TODAY

From then on, the city was known as the Republic of Rome.

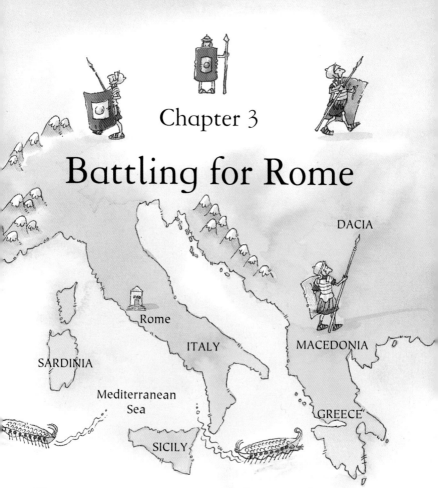

Chapter 3

Battling for Rome

Rome was now wealthy and strong. With its army, it didn't take long to seize control of the areas around it. Soon, the Romans ruled all of Italy and Rome became Italy's capital city.

But it wasn't so easy to *keep* things under control. The Romans were constantly being attacked by a Northern European tribe known as the Gauls.

The Gauls were ferocious fighters. After one battle, they chased the Roman soldiers back to Rome itself. The Gauls poured through the streets, looting and burning. The Romans retreated to the Capitol hill.

The Capitol was well defended, but the Gauls had a plan. One night, they crept silently up the hill, meaning to attack under cover of darkness. Suddenly, there was an ear-splitting screech.

Squaawk!

The Gauls had woken the sacred geese who lived in the gardens around the temple of Jupiter. The noise brought the Romans running and the Capitol was saved.

Eventually, the Romans defeated the Gauls and conquered most of the lands around the Mediterranean Sea, too. This meant Rome was more than a capital city. It was now the head of an empire.

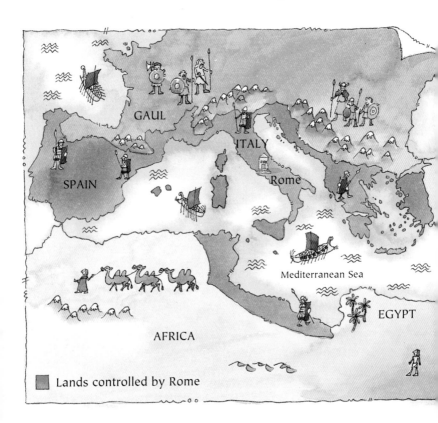

Lands controlled by Rome

Riches poured in from across the empire – gold, silver, jewels and slaves. This wealth helped to pay for many new buildings and monuments in Rome.

But, as the empire grew, there were arguments about how to run things. Fights broke out between powerful senators supported by different parts of the army. In the end, a general named Sulla seized power and made himself dictator.

Sulla was anxious to keep his hold on power. He killed or banished anyone he suspected of plotting against him – including an ambitious young man named Julius Caesar.

Caesar was sent away from Rome and joined the army. When Sulla died, he came back and worked his way up to become one of the city's most powerful men. Then, he was made Governor of Gaul. Helped by loyal soldiers, he put down rebels and conquered new lands.

The senators were horrified by Caesar's growing power and refused to obey him. In reply, he marched his army into Italy. The Senate's forces were no match for Caesar's loyal troops. And he didn't stop there. He went off to win more battles in Spain, Egypt and Asia.

I came, I saw, I conquered!

When Caesar got back, he was made Rome's new dictator. But the senators resented his king-like power and plotted against him. Soon after returning home, Caesar was stabbed to death.

Rome was plunged into chaos, as different groups within the city battled to take control. For twenty years, there was bitter fighting across Italy.

Finally, a new leader appeared – Octavian, Caesar's adopted son. He avenged the death of his father and defeated his rivals, including the Roman general Antony and the Egyptian queen Cleopatra.

Some senators remained, but Octavian was in charge. He made himself emperor and took the new name Augustus (meaning "noble").

Everyone seemed to like the new emperor. Despite his grand title, he lived with his family in an ordinary house. He spent his time improving Rome, overseeing new buildings and pipelines, known as aqueducts, which brought fresh water into the city.

At last, after hundreds of years of war and fighting, Rome had found peace again.

Chapter 4

Life in Rome

By the year 1, Rome had around a million residents. Crowds filled the city's great marketplace and narrow streets. In fact, the streets were so busy that vehicles were banned during the day.

The people of Rome were a mixed bunch. At the top of society stood the rich, powerful families known as patricians. Then there were the ordinary citizens.

At the bottom of the heap came the slaves. Unlike citizens, they had few rights. They weren't even allowed to wear togas – traditional Roman robes.

35

Patrician families lived in luxurious houses with running water and underfloor heating, and dozens of slaves to do their cooking and cleaning.

The women spent a lot of time styling their hair and organizing dinner parties.

A grand dinner involved dozens of dishes – from fried fish and roasted boar to delicacies such as peacock brains and stuffed dormice.

Diners lay on couches and ate with their fingers, while slaves waited on them and played music to keep everyone entertained.

But life wasn't all lounging around. Many Patrician men worked in the Senate or the army. They were also expected to help poor relations and former slaves.

Children from wealthy families went to school to learn to read and write.

As they got older, most girls left to get married. But boys stayed on to study speech making. This was vital if they wanted to go into politics.

After lessons, they played "catch" or challenged each other to games of marbles. Boys fought mock battles with wooden swords, while girls cradled toy dolls.

Ordinary citizens lived much less comfortably. Most rented small, wooden apartments with no running water – they had to collect what they needed from public fountains. Usually, the whole family had to work long hours, children included.

At mealtimes, they ate simple food like porridge or stew. For the very poorest citizens, the government provided free bread.

Cooking was banned in apartments because it caused too many fires – so Rome had lots of snack shops. But many people ignored the ban...

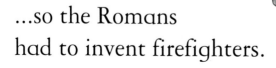

...so the Romans had to invent firefighters.

An important part of daily life
was going to the baths. All Romans,
rich or poor, tried to bathe several
times a week. Everyone used
the same pools, but there
were different hours for
men and women.

Hot pool

Sauna

Bathing
could take a
while. You began
in a steamy sauna.
Then you had a hot
soak, before relaxing
in a warm room. Last
came a bracing dip in
a chilly pool.

But there was no soap. The
Romans used oil instead, rubbing
it on and scraping
it off to get clean.

Warm room

Cold pool

On their days off, most Romans
went to watch the "Games" –
bloodthirsty contests between
trained fighters known as gladiators.

The biggest Games were held in
the Colosseum. This was a vast
arena of blood-stained sand, ringed
by 50,000 seats. It was opened by
the emperor Titus.

In front of a screaming audience,
the gladiators fought each other or
battled against wild animals.
Thousands died, though a lucky
few became rich and famous.

For added entertainment,
condemned prisoners were thrown
to the lions.

Religious festivals and holidays offered less gruesome fun, from games and races to drinking and dancing. And, every April, there were feasts and bonfires to celebrate the founding of Rome itself.

Chapter 5

Rome's emperors

Roman Empire

At its height, Rome controlled an empire stretching across half the known world. And one man, the emperor, was in charge of it all. That was fine if he was a good leader, like Augustus...

...but it wasn't so good if he was only interested in personal glory, or even insane – as Roman historians describe Caligula.

Caligula became emperor at the age of 25. At first, he was very popular. He was generous with money and kind to wrongdoers.

But not everyone approved of Caligula's lavish lifestyle. He spent a fortune on his palace.

When he turned a local temple
into his gatehouse, people began to
mutter that he had gone too far.

Then, after a sudden illness,
Caligula began behaving strangely.
He had fits of rage and turned very
cruel. Anyone who annoyed him
died a horrible death.

49

No one was safe. At one of the Games, Caligula decided there weren't enough gladiators. "Grab those spectators and make them take part!" he yelled.

The only thing Caligula really seemed to love was his horse. He gave it jewels and slaves, and even tried to make it a senator.

After four years, the Romans had had enough. One day, Caligula was walking down a corridor when his guards turned on him and stabbed him to death.

Barely ten years later, another terrible emperor took the throne – Nero. He was pushed into power by his mother, Agrippina, who hoped to make him do what she wanted. But Nero had other ideas.

I've got to get rid of her.

First, Nero tried to poison Agrippina. Then, he booby-trapped her bedroom with a collapsing ceiling. He even sent her to sea on a collapsible ship. But when the ship sank, she swam ashore.

In the end, Nero had to hire an assassin to finish her off.

With his mother out of the way, Nero could do what he liked – which was mostly sports and acting.

One year, Nero took part in the Olympic Games in Greece. No one dared to beat him, so Nero won all the prizes. He was so pleased, he didn't tax Greece for a year.

Nero also gave long shows. Nobody was allowed to leave before the end, though sometimes people pretended to die so they could be carried out.

Then, ten years into Nero's reign, disaster struck. One sweltering July night, a fire broke out in some shops near the Circus Maximus. The flames spread fast, until soon most of Rome was ablaze.

Nero was visiting the seaside at the time. Legend says he watched from a distance, happily playing a fiddle while Rome burned.

The fire lasted for nine days.
When it finally died out, two-thirds
of the city was smoking rubble.

Nero was delighted. He had been
trying to flatten part of Rome in
order to build a huge golden palace,
but the Senate had stopped him.
Now, the palace could go ahead –
leading people to gossip that Nero
had started the fire himself.

But Nero's hold on power was slipping. His senators and generals were plotting against him. Facing defeat, Nero committed suicide.

Luckily, Rome's emperors weren't all bad. Probably the most admired, after Augustus, was Trajan.

Trajan started life as a soldier. He was such a brilliant soldier that the emperor Nerva adopted him. And when Nerva died, Trajan inherited the throne.

To the Romans, Trajan was more than a ruler. He was a hero. He led his army into many battles, the most famous being in Dacia (now part of Romania).

The Dacians fought bravely, but Trajan defeated them. Dacia was forced to join the Roman empire, and Trajan's army returned to Rome loaded down with Dacian gold and silver.

Trajan used the gold to glorify the city, building a grand new marketplace. To remind people of his triumph, a marble pillar known as "Trajan's Column" was put up, carved with scenes of his victories.

By the time Trajan died, Rome was the head of an empire greater than any the world had ever seen. But it was not to last.

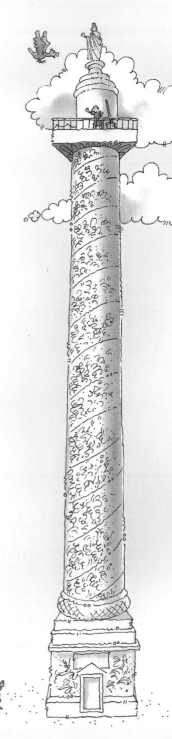

Chapter 5

Decline and fall

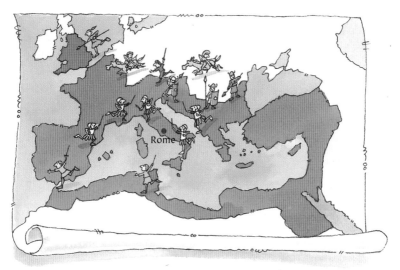

Rome

As the Roman empire got bigger, it also got harder to run. There were too many distant territories and borders to control. After years of chaos, the emperor Diocletian decided drastic measures were needed.

Diocletian divided the empire in two. A deputy would run the western half from Rome, while he ruled the eastern half from Turkey. Rome was no longer the capital of the world.

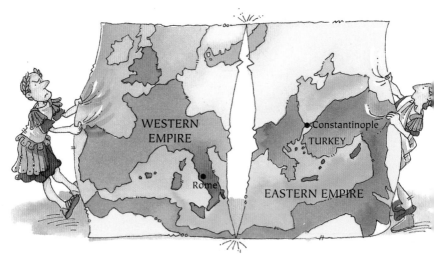

Rome was further overshadowed when the emperor Constantine created a new capital, Constantinople, in Turkey. The new city was built to rival Rome's wealth and magnificence.

In the west, the old Rome was under attack. German tribes known as Goths and Vandals ransacked the city and toppled its emperor. The western empire was over – although the eastern empire survived another thousand years.

But even today much of the old Rome still stands, from ancient aqueducts and temples to Trajan's monumental column and the vast, arched walls of the Colosseum.

TIMELINE

About 1000 BCE* The first people begin to settle on the Roman hills.

753 BCE According to legend, this is when Romulus founded Rome.

About 625 BCE This is when historians think Rome was founded.

600 BCE The Forum is built.

550 BCE The city walls are built.

510-509 BCE King Tarquin the Proud is exiled and Rome becomes a Republic.

509 BCE The temple on the Capitol Hill is dedicated to Jupiter.

About 390 BCE The Gauls attack Rome.

312 BCE The first aqueduct is built, to bring fresh water into the city.

222 BCE The Romans finally defeat the Gauls.

81 BCE Sulla makes himself dictator of Rome.

45 BCE Julius Caesar becomes dictator.

44 BCE Julius Caesar is assassinated.

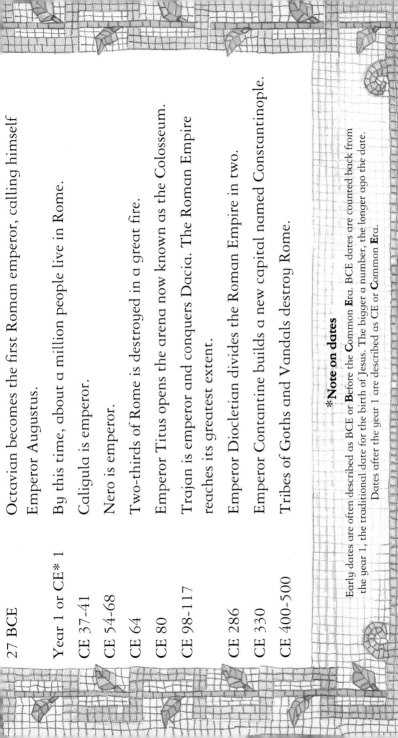

27 BCE	Octavian becomes the first Roman emperor, calling himself Emperor Augustus.
Year 1 or CE* 1	By this time, about a million people live in Rome.
CE 37-41	Caligula is emperor.
CE 54-68	Nero is emperor.
CE 64	Two-thirds of Rome is destroyed in a great fire.
CE 80	Emperor Titus opens the arena now known as the Colosseum.
CE 98-117	Trajan is emperor and conquers Dacia. The Roman Empire reaches its greatest extent.
CE 286	Emperor Diocletian divides the Roman Empire in two.
CE 330	Emperor Contantine builds a new capital named Constantinople.
CE 400-500	Tribes of Goths and Vandals destroy Rome.

*Note on dates

Early dates are often described as BCE or **B**efore the **C**ommon **E**ra. BCE dates are counted back from the year 1, the traditional date for the birth of Jesus. The bigger a number, the longer ago the date.

Dates after the year 1 are described as CE or **C**ommon **E**ra.

Series editor: Lesley Sims

With thanks to Will Sims, aged 7,
for his comments and suggestions

Designed by Natacha Goransky
Cover design by Russell Punter

Internet links

For links to some fun websites about Rome,
go to the Usborne Quicklinks Website at
www.usborne-quicklinks.com
and type the keywords **YR Rome**.

Please note that Usborne Publishing cannot
be responsible for the content of any website
other than its own.